I0463229

BEYOND BILLING

FIVE STEPS TO BECOMING A SUCCESSFUL TECHNOLOGY CONSULTANT

RAVI GANGA

ISBN: 1463720041
ISBN-13: 9781463720049
Library of Congress Control Number: 2011912380
CreateSpace Independent Publishing Platform
North Charleston, SC

To Anitha - my consultant of unconditional
love and grace.

To Dad and Amma – thank you.

CONTENTS

INTRODUCTION

Of the fifteen years I have spent in the IT consulting industry, about half the time has been spent on learning the tricks of the trade. I could have avoided the initial naivety and lack of direction had I asked the right questions and had a mentor who could have answered them. However, the vicissitudes of my journey as a consultant have resulted in this book, a new reality outlining five steps that a technology consultant can add to his day-to-day life and make the most of the opportunities around him.

Many years ago, I was consulting for a client in North Carolina, when the engagement manager on the account called and suggested I delay my upcoming trip to India by a week. We both knew the importance of the trip. My fiancée-to-be and I were counting the days toward our engagement ceremony (which in India is consummated by friends, family, and traditional rituals), so it was hard to fathom the exact reason behind his request.

It turned out that one more week of work would have beefed up his numbers, although that hadn't occurred to me at that point. I went ahead with the trip as scheduled, but ultimately lost out on the opportunity to work for the client again. This incident kick-started a series of events that taught me some very important lessons. And these events have ranged from extreme frustrations to unexpected successes.

Six years later, I am writing this book to sum up my experience in five important steps for a consultant to go beyond the primordial instincts of treating every assignment as a billing exercise, irrespective of whether it was forced or conceived in the minds of every consultant. This is not to say that every company or consultant goes with the billing mindset, but the business of technology consulting is such that it invariably ends with equating productivity to the dollars earned by the consultant, minus his salary.

This book doesn't debate the integrity of the technology-consulting business models. To be fair to any consulting shop—if you cut to the chase of strategies, offerings, frameworks, and delivery models—the end products are always humans (consultants) who are the prima facie of any engagement. So, this book is about the consultant himself, the challenges, the opportunities, and a method for dealing with the troughs and going beyond archaic "billing" and "thick-skin" perspectives.

Finally what we end up with is a value system for the consultant that is an artifact of awareness, opportunities, infinite possibilities, and the ability to enjoy and celebrate successes. I have strictly kept the scope of this book to the technology (IT) consulting business although it would be fair to say that this book will prove useful to consultants and professionals of all varieties.

In this book, a "consultant" can be just about anybody who works on a billable model for a client. They can vary in size and shape. Also, for the sake of convenience, the book refers to the consultant using the masculine gender; it goes without saying that the intention is to make this book purposeful for all readers irrespective of their gender. I hope you enjoy what you read in the next few chapters and that this book helps you make the best out of your consulting life, in any capacity or role.

Disclaimer: The book is presented solely for educational purposes. The characters, stories and entities are entirely fictional. Neither the author nor the publisher shall be held liable or responsible to any person or entity with respect to any loss or incidental or consequential damages caused, or alleged to have been caused, directly or indirectly, by the information contained herein.

BEYOND BILLING:

THE TECHNOLOGY CONSULTANT

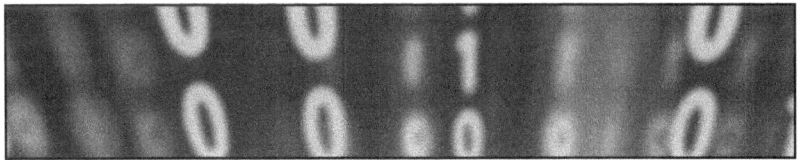

THE PYRAMID OF EXPECTATIONS

A cross the globe, millions of consultants today serve in the IT consulting industry worth billions of dollars. Almost all of these consultants work toward the same goal. Using specialized skills as individuals or as a group, they help businesses and consumers bridge the demands of the digital age. Across several enterprises and markets and industries, consultants work with their clients to solve the problems of exponential changes in technology, new methods of innovation, and constant refinement of business processes.

Unlike consultants in other fields—even when compared to broad areas of other types of consulting—technology consultants vary in many aspects. Seasoned consultants run their own small niche firms. Consultants work for high-end consulting shops providing professional services that support products. And millions of workers in developing countries like India work on outsourced IT projects. Businesses across the globe employ different types of vendors providing IT consultancy services to suit their different needs across the board, but with the same underlying theme and expectations. These expectations can be represented by the following pyramid:

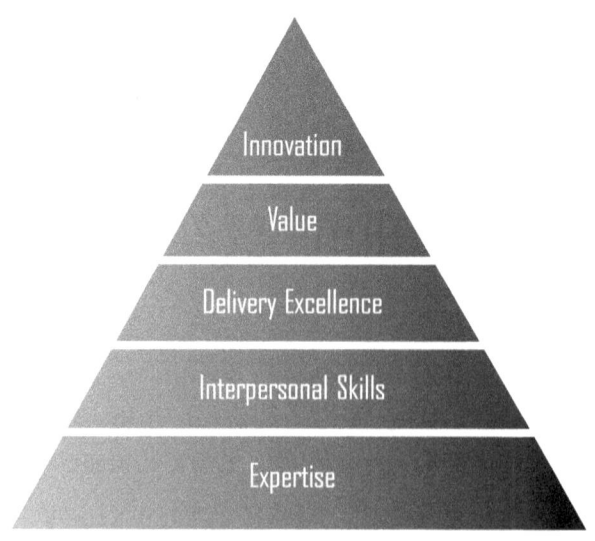

Referring to the pyramid, consultants usually end up delivering against the following expectations, with each expectation forming the basis for the one above it:

1. **Expertise**: The most basic of expectations. The consultant should bring to the table a set of technical skillsets that allow him to fulfill his role as a specialist. Along with his strong technical expertise, the consultant comes with strong problem-solving skills, a given in technology professionals.

2. **Interpersonal skills**: Once the expertise need is met, it is expected that the consultant has a personality that is influential across the different mix of audiences he comes in contact with. The consultant might be a geek obsessed with the workings of technology, but is versatile enough to present and negotiate with nontechnical professionals.

3. **Delivery excellence**: Once the expertise and soft skills are validated, the expectation moves up to excellence in delivery. The expectation now is that the consultant does a no-nonsense job of working well within the timelines, is calm and poised under challenging circumstances, and does an excellent job of going above and beyond just meeting his deliverables.

4. **Value**: Once the consultant meets the basic expectations, clients look for value. The consultant must bring value for money. Because consultants are often paid at a higher rate than some full-time

employees are, or because business conditions necessitate offshoring as a cost-saving measure, it is expected that a consultant must implicitly prove his value every day.

5. **Innovation**: This factor often goes unnoticed. Clients expect consultants to contribute to the rising arc of meeting business demands, keeping them informed on better ways of doing things in the most creative manner. Innovating while saving costs and bringing value should be the highest endeavor of consultants.

It is not hard to notice that meeting all of these expectations and having a decent work–life balance can be a daunting task. However, to remind the reader, the premise of this book is that all these challenges can be turned into opportunities for growth that potentially lead to several satisfying possibilities.

PITFALLS AND GAINS

Several years ago, I was sitting in a secluded boarding area in the Cincinnati airport cursing my yet-again delayed flight and mentally picking the best place to eat. To top it off, I had the most awful experience with a client who couldn't possibly understand the difference between two very different platforms. Also, it had been a couple of weeks since I had eaten a decent homemade meal, and the proposition of another slice of pizza inspired some deep questions.

How did I land here?

Fate. I could have been the writer eating three or more homemade meals a day listening to Bollywood songs during breaks.

Exactly when did I turn into a consultant?

There was no "I have a dream. I am going to be a great consultant" moment either.

What can I do to improve my career?

I will answer that after that slice of spinach and garlic staring at me from Sbarro's.

Almost every consultant reaches a point where he starts to question his very making as a consultant. In my own career, I have had a lot of demoralizing experiences and there were several attempts to get out of the tiring nature of a consulting job. In terms of understanding the pitfalls, it is useful to get this perspective from a frustrated consultant:

1. **Expertise**: I need to keep my skills updated. Learning new skills requires time and energy outside of my day-to-day work. The pace of technology innovation is such that I can never claim to be a guru in any subject.

2. **Interpersonal skills**: I try my best to find common ground among the client contacts, my team, and various other stakeholders. I cannot claim responsibility for politics and differences of opinions.

3. **Delivery excellence**: Clients have this insatiable lust for doing more with less. The more efficient I become, the more demanding my clients become. I would rather keep their expectations low.

4. **Value**: At the end of the day, I strive to achieve maximum value for myself and for the client. However, there is always a clash of expectations. My client sometimes thinks I am a salesman, and my employer expects I should bring in more value.

5. **Innovation**: It is hard enough to keep up with my skillsets, keeping the client happy, and meeting my deliverables. My top priority is just to get my job done.

There are also consultants of a different breed, the ones who are content, happy, and extremely successful in their careers. The mind-set of such consultants tells a different story:

1. **Expertise**: My eyes and ears are always open for the new things that are happening in my specialty. I don't make any special effort to keep myself updated; things come to me. The client identifies me with a core skill, and I am happy to be approached in all aspects pertaining to that skill.

2. **Interpersonal skills**: The client sees me as a trusted advisor and a best friend in helping make his endeavors successful. I don't necessarily have to

create a common ground between different types of audiences; however, it is clear that the client is aware of my intentions.

3. **Delivery excellence**: Being the client's trusted advisor, the client understands that I will try my best to rise to the challenges and deliver in time, to the best of my abilities. I always set clear expectations and goals with the client, and the client appreciates my transparency.

4. **Value**: To me, value means maximum bang for the client's buck. Every action that I take and every word I speak centers around value. I go "beyond billing."

5. **Innovation**: Innovation is not just the expertise I bring to the table, but it is also about my everyday interactions with the client. The more disciplined my execution, interpersonal skills, delivery and value, the more innovation I deliver.

The purpose of this book is to expand the consultant's awareness to help him shift from the place of stress and frustration to the other end of the spectrum, where the consultant learns a new approach to fulfilling his desires and create opportunities that help him become more successful. And while doing so, the consultant goes beyond treating his client engagements as just a billing exercise. He goes *beyond billing* and wins.

BEYOND BILLING:
A NEW REALITY

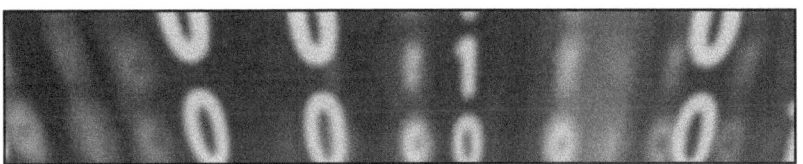

CREATING A NEW REALITY

Several years ago, working as an Infrastructure Architect consultant for a client, I was fated to work for a director who at once put me at unease. Notwithstanding the frequent checkpoint meetings laced with questions ranging from "Weren't you supposed to finish that yesterday?" to "I would like to see the proof of concept in the next few hours," it was soon becoming a living hell.

Six weeks into the assignment, with added pressure from an uncooperative offshore team and the stress of having moved to a crowded metropolis from the countryside of North Carolina, I decided to look for a different assignment. (We will call the director "Steve" for reference.) Steve apparently got wind of this. He often found me missing at my desk. On a cold March afternoon, he sent one of his team members with a verbal memo: Finish configuring the product I was assigned that week or I don't have to bother coming in the next day. Shocked, I had to decide between walking away from this situation once for all and giving this product one last try after a month-long struggle.

It was only 2:00 in the afternoon, so I decided to pursue configuring the product—one last time. By 9:30 that night, I had finished. In delirious joy, I sent an e-mail to Steve and copied a bunch of others with screenshots politely expressing my rage and silently vowed not to come back again.

The next morning I showed up but had received no replies of "thanks" or "well done." Instead, several more tasks around the same product were laid out with manageable timelines, this time. For reasons unknown to me, I impulsively walked into Steve's office with the intention of confronting him. Unsure of what I had to say, Steve acted nonchalant when I pressed him to show at least a decent bit of appreciation. Finally, he gave in, in his thick New York accent, "This is exactly what I want to see from you—lots of passion and communication."

Confused, I went back to my desk wondering if I had misread the whole situation. In the next few months, my relationship with Steve grew stronger to the point that he tried his best to keep me on his team even after the contract expired and the project in context ended.

If we could map this situation to the *Pyramid of Expectations*, my initial flaws in interacting with Steve led him to believe the following:

1. **Expertise**: Ravi is good enough to do the job but doesn't seem focused.

2. **Interpersonal skills**: I want him to talk to me eye to eye, but he seems lost every time.

3. **Delivery excellence**: I don't mind his telling me about the roadblocks he has been facing, but he just doesn't seem interested in finishing his tasks.

4. **Value**: I cannot quantify the value he brings to the table.

5. **Innovation**: I am confident that a good replacement will add more value and help my project succeed.

Steve's few words of feedback instantly gave me the vision of a new reality, and I went about changing my interaction with him by redefining how I align my work with his *Pyramid of Expectations*:

1. **Expertise**: I should demonstrate not only my core skills but also my understanding of the breadth and depth of Steve's tasks.

2. **Interpersonal skills**: I can't turn myself into a flamboyant Yankee just to make Steve happy, but I can do a better job of being honest, upfront and precise in every interaction.

3. **Delivery excellence**: I should be demonstrative of going above and beyond in meeting my deliverables, with integrity and passion. I should effectively communicate any roadblocks.

4. **Value**: I shouldn't take my job for granted and should demonstrate the unique technical and product insights I bring to Steve's projects. My most important task is making Steve successful.

5. **Innovation**: I should partner with the client in thinking two steps ahead and anticipating risks and opportunities for success.

CHARACTERISTICS OF A NEW REALITY

My objective in sharing the aforementioned scenario is to paint the genesis of a new reality that we will discuss going forward. Obviously, there are clients who are totally unappreciative of any sincere efforts. And there are clients who are relatively easy to work with, with whom consultants can seamlessly prove their worth.

Having said that, it is imperative to treat any consulting engagement with a reality that is borne out of unchanging integrity and one that successfully meets the challenges presented by the *Pyramid of Expectations*. Armed with this new awareness, it helps consultants to deal with stressful unknowns by inculcating the following characteristics in their day-to-day assignments:

1. **Expertise**: I value what I bring to the table and work hard in keeping up with changes and progress in my areas of expertise. My expertise is the defining benchmark of my identity as a consultant.

2. **Interpersonal skills**: I am a consultant, which means that every interaction should have an equal measure of connecting with the client and his priorities and demonstrating the highest professional standards.

3. **Delivery excellence**: The ever-changing dynamics of this world always point to doing more with less. I should be a proponent of polishing my delivery and being transparent about meeting the project timelines.

4. **Value**: The value I bring to the table is apparent from day one. My mission is to showcase my expertise and demonstrate the effectiveness with which I deliver. By doing so, I implicitly bring value to the table.

5. **Innovation**: By bringing my core expertise and efficient delivery to the client, I open doors and opportunities to align Technology with the client's priorities and limitations.

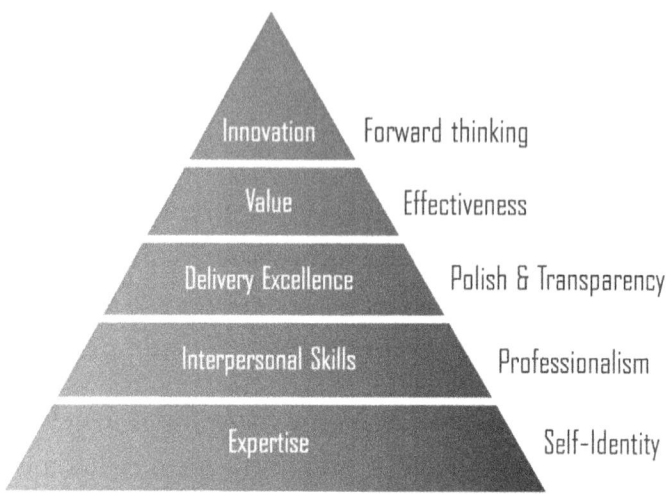

Finally, meeting the *Pyramid of Expectations* with a new reality can be helpful only once the consultant knows how to map this new perspective to a series of practical steps. The next chapters offer a five-step plan for implementing this novel reality in ways that fulfill the mission of this book, which is to go *beyond billing*.

STEP 1: PROFILE YOUR CLIENT

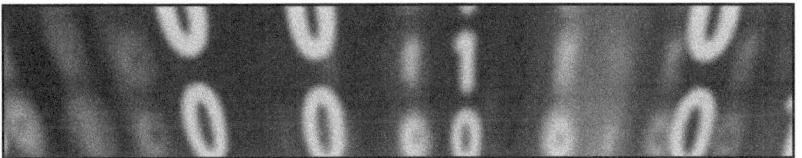

BROADENING THE HORIZON

Several years ago, when I applied for a position in a product division of a huge software company, the first impression the hiring manager got from my "hard-core consultant" résumé was the breadth of the listed technologies and clientele, and the shallowness of each assignment. "Exactly what have you shipped so far?" was a blunt but legitimate question. Not knowing what to answer, I somehow managed to show him the good side of my consulting experience but ultimately lost out in the future rounds.

On further introspection and counseling from mentors, it was apparent that my résumé actually reflected the truth I heard from the hiring manager. Between running from one client to the other and nicely settling as an expert across a set of technologies, I could not comprehend the bigger picture. It was clear that to make the leap to the next career level by transforming my diverse experience into something more valuable, I had to widen the scope of my daily livelihood.

This can be a tricky concept to understand, but ultimately success in any field is achieved only by broadening the number of elements an individual is capable of impacting and adding value to, every day. And this is exactly the purpose of this step—*profiling your client.*

The word *profile* has many interpretations, but it comes down to answering the following questions about the client. (For the purposes of keeping it simple, the references to "organization" point to the division/business unit/IT group the consultant reports to at the client site.)

1. **Success factor:** What does the organization do for a living, and what makes it successful?

2. **Contribution:** How does this organization contribute to the overall IT organization?

3. **Key stakeholders:** Who are the key stakeholders and decision makers in the organization?

4. **Priorities:** What are the IT priorities of my client's business?

5. **Performance:** As a company, how is it fairing in the market?

6. **Competition:** How are the client's competitors innovating in the technology space?

From the consultant's standpoint, awareness of these questions can add tremendous insight into how he approaches any and every client situation. As an example: An Architect consultant is brought onboard for a four-week engagement to validate a technology platform and perform a proof of concept for the content management division of a bank. If the Architect consultant takes his time to profile this client, he might end up with the following insights:

The *success* of this organization depends on how well the organization manages the intellectual assets of the bank and *contributes* to the overall effectiveness of bulging information properties and business processes year after year. The **key stakeholders** in this group have been assigned the responsibility of seamlessly migrating from platform X to platform Y without affecting the IT *priority* of business continuity. A successful migration to this new platform will increase the efficiency and *performance* of the field agents and will help the bank innovate against *competition* Z.

It is clear now that asking these questions can lead to widening the horizons from where the consultant can take meaningful strides toward meeting the *Pyramid of Expectations*:

1. **Expertise**: I understand the criticality of my expertise to client's success. I am inspired to learn more.

2. **Interpersonal skills**: I understand the politics of my client's business. From the knowledge I have gained from profiling the client, my conversations will center on how well I understand the client's priorities.

3. **Delivery excellence**: Good relationships and awareness help shape deliverables that are well received by the client.

4. **Value**: From my observations of key stakeholders, understanding of priorities, and criticality of my endeavor, I go beyond billing and help the client see value in my service daily.

5. **Innovation**: I understand the competition, market trends, and overall goals of the client. I am intimately involved in going beyond my deliverables and speaking the language of innovation.

The questions asked in the beginning of this chapter are just the tip of the iceberg. And the value derived from *profiling* varies according to the length of the project and the role of the consultant, but we can all agree that it goes a long way in making the consultant's job much more meaningful. From the Architect consultant example earlier, instead of restricting his experience at the bank to "migration of platform X to Y," it can now read as "validation of content management platform migration by delivering a proof of concept that imbibed the best of industry standards by taking into account the bank's IT and business priorities."

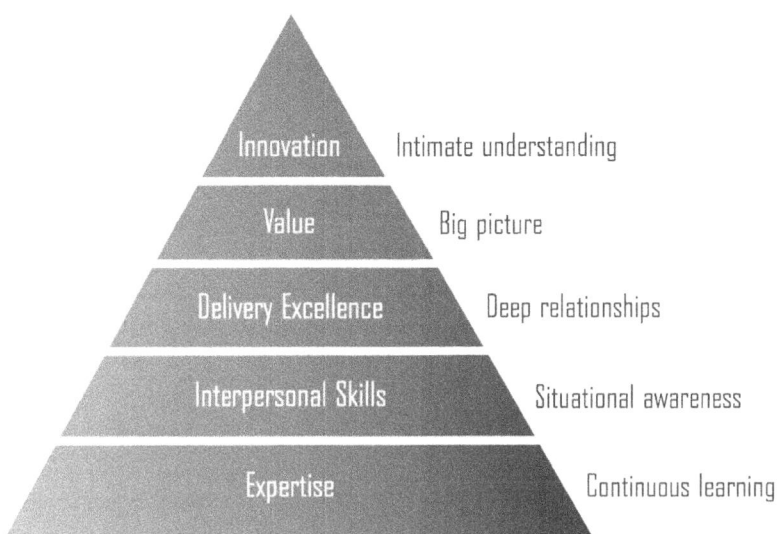

Innovation — Intimate understanding

Value — Big picture

Delivery Excellence — Deep relationships

Interpersonal Skills — Situational awareness

Expertise — Continuous learning

STEP 2:

USE YOUR ENTREPRENEURIAL SPIRIT

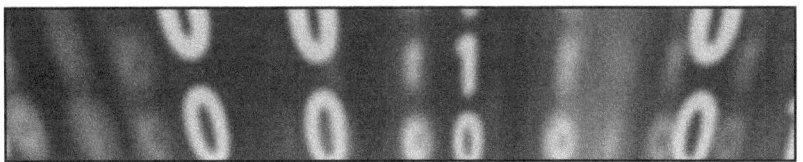

RUNNING YOUR BUSINESS

Eating my lunch sitting in an open space on a cold Manhattan afternoon, the phone rang and I had to choose between eating in peace and answering the call. I chose the latter and heard a worried tone on the other end.

"This consulting thing is a load of b—! I'd rather be back to working for that insurance company that I quit for this."

21

Vladimir's emotions were running high after his manager at a leading consulting firm failed to appreciate his efforts. Vladimir was confident that he did everything right. He was able to show value to the client in a short timeframe, rescued a grim project situation, and got his contract extended for a good six more months.

"What does your account team think of your achievements?" I asked curiously.

"What do you mean? The engagement manager hardly picks up the phone," came back an unexcited reply.

"Do you know who manages the client account besides you and other consultants"? I quizzed further.

"Yes, I met some in one of those happy hour team events, but who cares?" Vladimir argued.

After some more of those annoying questions, I figured that although Vladimir had done a great job in showcasing his value and expertise to his client, he lacked awareness of his behind-the-scenes colleagues who run the show, and he might have even rubbed some of them the wrong way. These folks can include the engagement managers, delivery leads, account and sales execs who are responsible for the overall sales, delivery, and health of the business.

In Vladimir's case, he thought he had done an exceedingly good job for his client. He got great utilization and client satisfaction, yet he found a boss who thought he was only doing "OK". Unfortunately for Vladimir, he failed to realize the value of integrating with the rest of the key stakeholders who drive a consulting engagement. However, one can reckon that things would have been different had Vladimir been an entrepreneur or a freelancer running his own consulting gig.

Most often consultants treat consulting engagements as a normal salaried job working for some employer, not appreciating the work that goes into finding an IT services opportunity in a highly competitive environment. The truth of the matter is, in a consultant's job, almost everyone he encounters is a client. Not a client in the sense of keeping everyone happy, but a client in the sense of integrating and understanding the holistic and overall objectives of the client's account.

In Vladimir's case, he invested all of his energies in ensuring the client contact he worked for is happy and satisfied—and in the process, some of his actions didn't go down well with some of his colleagues, which impacted some key revenue generating opportunities.

EVERYONE IS A CLIENT

The truth about technology consulting, considering the constant flux of technology decision making and the related dynamics of cost and governance, is that it makes a technology consultant's job a delicate thread, full of uncertainty. On the one hand, the consultant deals with climbing the client's *Pyramid of Expectations*; on the other hand, he faces numerous other stakeholders who have their own vested interests. Technically, the larger the client account, the larger the number of important contacts. In addition, the more uncertainties a consultant deals with, the more he is liable to integrate with other stakeholders in the account.

In a business model that involves a body of work that makes use of the intellectual and interpersonal skills, everyone a consultant comes in contact with is a client. The consultant has to look at his job as running his business like an *entrepreneur*. It cannot be any other way, as the variables in a consulting engagement are constantly changing.

A consultant's manager is often entrusted with a utilization target for his group; a freelance consultant has to ensure he integrates with his partners to ensure repeat work from the client. An account executive wants to maximize his sales, so a selfish consultant refusing to share his expertise and refusing to integrate with the extended team is an impediment to success. The chain of dependency is complex, and a consultant should do his part in keeping it together.

Now, an efficient consultant meets this objective by using his entrepreneurial instincts with the knowledge that his best chance at success is not just from understanding the nitty-gritties of the client objectives, but by also recognizing that his actions have an impact on the entire business.

So, how does a consultant with this awareness realize the *Pyramid of Expectations*?

1. **Expertise**: My expertise is realized not only through my technical skills. It is most importantly, realized through how well I present a unified image of my employer's services at the client site.

2. **Interpersonal skills**: My every action is a collective representation of the vision and strategy of the company or firm that I represent. My client doesn't receive conflicting ideas of the business I represent.

3. **Delivery excellence**: My deliverables have visibility across the board. My team understands how well I am contributing to the overall goals.

4. **Value**: I bring value to the client and my extended team by keeping the best interests of both parties and having won the trust of all.

5. **Innovation**: Acting as the common bridge across a broad spectrum of individuals and their interests, I help lead the innovation for all stakeholders.

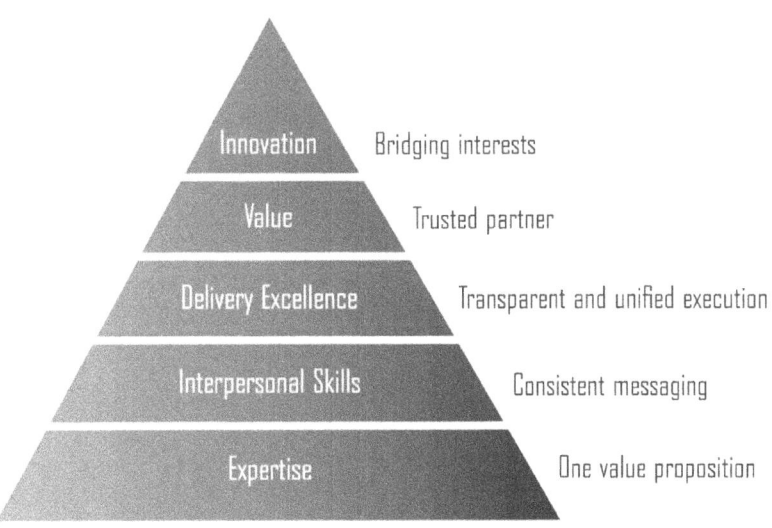

Innovation	Bridging interests
Value	Trusted partner
Delivery Excellence	Transparent and unified execution
Interpersonal Skills	Consistent messaging
Expertise	One value proposition

STEP 3:
POLISH YOUR EXECUTION

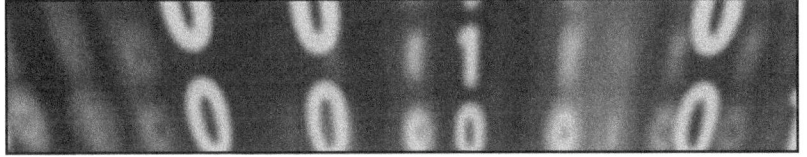

GARNISHING YOUR DISH

Gordon Eubanks once said, "Strategy gets you on the playing field, but execution pays the bills." Business schools can dedicate a whole semester to the numerous definitions of execution, but in a consultant's world, it's simple: climb the *Pyramid of Expectations* every day but do so in a manner that leaves a lasting impression.

It is safe to assume that at some point most consultants have worn the hat of a geek. While creating logic, solving analytical problems, or even solving complex business-technical challenges, the consultant is considered at most times a technical resource or a coordinator of technical artifacts. With that tag comes the stereotyping that has the following impressions:

1. Most consultants do not possess skills in addressing diverse audiences and speaking the language of the client and stakeholders.

2. Consultants can at best be expected to solve problems. Articulating value propositions, embracing the complexity of business expectations and delivering pinpoint messages is too much to expect from a consultant.

3. Most consultants do a good technical job, but what is missing is the art of managing deep personal relationships.

4. Most often consultants are so passionate about technology they fail to connect with the critical elements of a client's business.

5. Some consultants are like chefs who do a great cooking job but forget to put the food on an attractive plate and garnish it with the proper ingredients.

Many people unconsciously believe these impressions of Technology consultants. There are always some emphasis on soft skills, language, and overall client-facing etiquette, but nowhere do you come across a course that talks about polishing a consultant's execution.

The word *polish,* used in the context of a personality, might point to someone having an arresting personality by virtue of his or her exemplary behavior or etiquette. Put in the context of execution, polish is about the display put on by the consultant while meeting the *Pyramid of Expectations.* One can turn around the unconscious beliefs about Technology consultants by reversing them and demonstrating that to the client during the length of the project and beyond. Mainly, the following are the attributes of a consultant who executes with polish, once the unconscious impressions are reversed:

1. The consultant is not a Jack Welch or a Shakespeare but does a decent job of understanding and mimicking some of the cultural idiosyncrasies of his client.

2. The consultant has the ability to think clearly, beyond just accomplishing his tasks and solving problems. He has the innate ability to articulate the value of his work, the company, and his client's mission. The consultant is a fearless and passionate presenter.

3. The consultant strives to know his clients at a personal level. The consultant truly goes *beyond billing* by giving his time, energy, and effort to make a difference to his client.

4. The consultant is not just a work horse. He can switch from talking about technology to the client's overall vision to sports to hot topics of the day without apprehension. The consultant, however, is careful and knows his boundaries.

5. Whether the consultant writes an e-mail, answers a question, or delivers a report, he exhibits professionalism, character, and leaves a stamp of his class.

To be fair, all these qualities emerge once a consultant has gone through several engagements, but today is a day when you can start to execute with more polish and finesse. How does a consultant with polish in execution meet the *Pyramid of Expectations*?

1. **Expertise**: My expertise is not limited to technical skillsets, but it is about presenting a complete package that leaves a lasting impression.

2. **Interpersonal skills**: My every action has a touch of personal attention and an intention to deeply relate to the client. The client remembers me as he reflects on the artifacts I have contributed to.

3. **Delivery excellence**: By adding personal and professional touch to my deliverables, I leave a lasting impression on the client. I do so by knowing that good presentation can make a big difference in the end.

4. **Value**: The client personally relates to me and appreciates my ability to clearly articulate simple and complex situations. I bring value by being professional and concise in my expressions.

5. **Innovation**: I save my client's business cycles with my clear thinking, professionalism, and ability to relate to people at both personal and professional levels. The saved cycles open the opportunities for innovation and success.

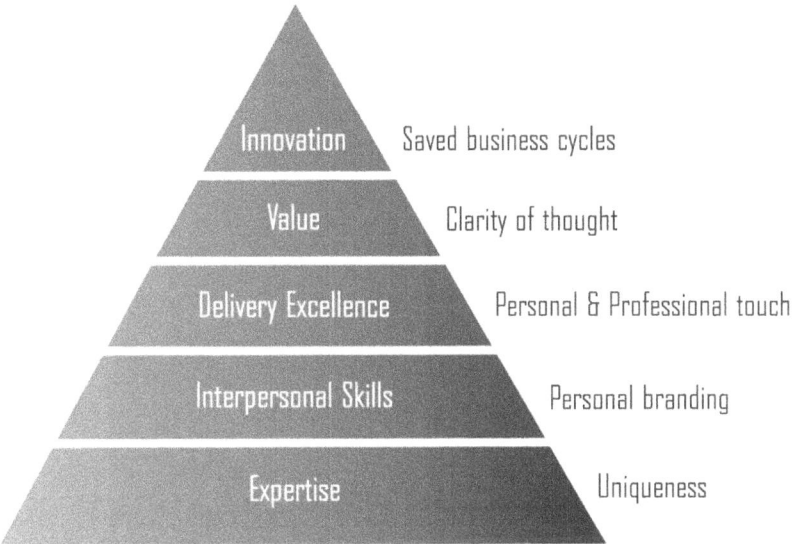

STEP 4:
GO SOCIAL WITH YOUR EXPERTISE

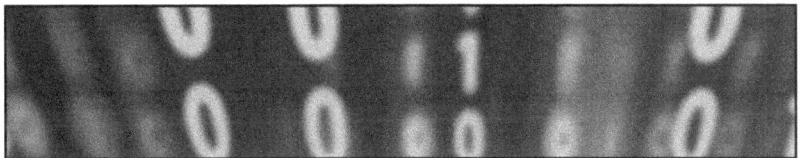

TRANSCENDING WORK

Albert Einstein once said, "Any man who reads too much and uses his own brain too little falls into lazy habits of thinking." This is most relevant to a consultant's lifestyle. Most consultants spend their busy schedule doing a good job for the client, learning new skills, and stepping into the unknown alleys of career development. Some consultants blog their experience, some create intellectual property, some move to the next lucrative spot in their careers. However, most don't stop and go beyond their routines.

So, how does a consultant climb the *Pyramid of Expectations* even before he has met the client? He does so by the sheer force of his reputation, which can be sought by search engines and social networking sites, sometimes revealing more about the consultant before he gets a chance to say hello. In the increasingly social world of ours, a consultant who creates his niche outside of his work by sharing expertise and gaining recognition in the cyber-world ensures his climbing of the *Pyramid of Expectations* to be easier and richer in returns than the ones who don't.

It's not just the cyber-social aspect that matters. A consultant with rich experiences in numerous client situations, businesses, technologies, and places is a rich resource of adaptability, business acumen, and soft skills, which sets him apart from his peers. The consultant is simultaneously an entrepreneur and a knowledge worker billed by the hour and sharing this guile in areas and situations outside of day-to-day responsibilities further enhances the consultant's value.

The theory behind going *social with your expertise* is to conceive a new model of consultant's expertise. In this model, the consultant is aware of the following components that shape his career:

1. *My skills are not mine alone.* I owe my expertise to the vast experiences of client situations and people who have directly or indirectly influenced my abilities.

2. *I believe in sharing my expertise.* When I share, I learn from other individuals and my time and resources are used to increase awareness on many subjects.

3. *Learning and teaching are two sides of the same coin.* When I learn something new or hit upon an insight, it is most beneficial when I put them to use in practical situations. This is also true when it comes to teaching and mentoring others.

4. *I have an open mind.* I appreciate the Buddhist saying: "When you meet Buddha on the road, kill him." Knowledge and its nirvana have boundaries that can never be touched. Every client situation, every mentoring and sharing opportunity expands my awareness.

Finally, with this reality and novel perception, the consultant exhibits the qualities of an open-minded individual and is looked upon by his clients, colleagues and peers as an individual with qualities of a defenseless and an unbiased expert, willing to learn and share his expertise.

So, how does this step of going truly social with expertise help the consultant climb the *Pyramid of Expectations?*

1. **Expertise**: A look at my cyber-profile reveals my contribution to the community, and at a deeper level, I have a personality that reflects the qualities of an open mind.

2. **Interpersonal skills**: I believe in participation and collaboration over blithely demonstrating and debating what is right. When in challenging decision-making situations, I choose what is best for the client and learn what is right from others.

3. **Delivery excellence**: I look at my deliverables from the eyes of a student and teacher. As a student, I appreciate the uniqueness of every client situation; as a teacher, I leverage my past experience and expertise.

4. **Value**: I add value by leveraging my skills to the maximum benefit of my clients and do so in a manner that leaves footprints of my execution for future situations and opportunities.

5. **Innovation**: Being a sincere student and a giving teacher, I help clients innovate with my spontaneous insights and rich knowledge of dealing with complex situations.

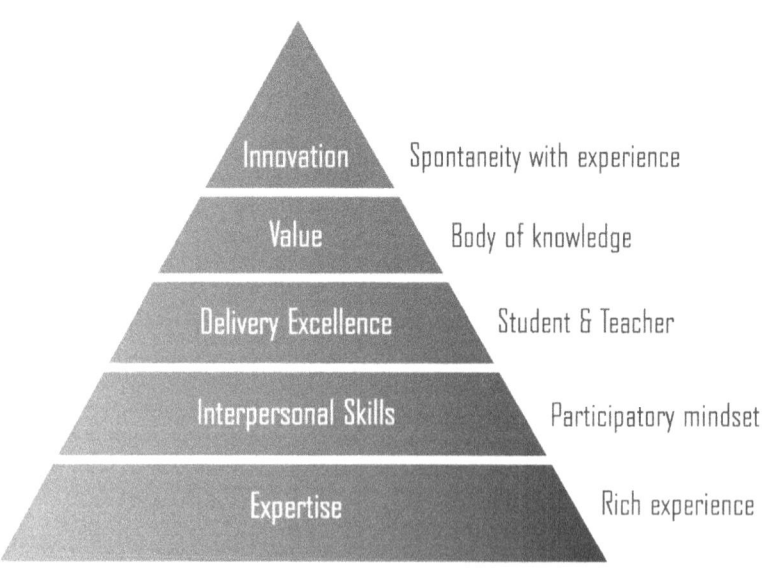

STEP 5:
CELEBRATE EVERYTHING

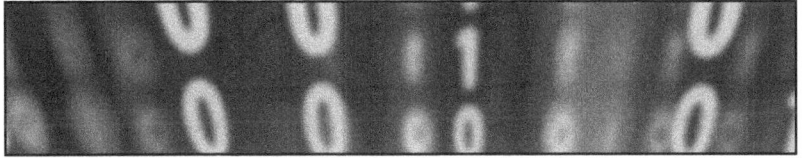

THE ART OF REJOICING

As we drove past several boulevards with spectacular trees and houses during the peak of summer in Danbury, Connecticut, my client boss quickly became wary of my rough driving. Five minutes into the drive, he admonished me like an older brother, and we quickly slipped into swapping stories of growing up in New England versus the metros of India and how it affected our respective driving habits. (We will call the client–boss "Charles" for reference).

I was taking Charles out for lunch to mark the end of my first year with his team. I had developed a deep friendly relationship with him built on long meaningful conversations that usually ended with Charles's recounting of his life lessons. I enjoyed listening to him but also ensured I did a stellar job for his team. As we sat across each other in the Indian restaurant, I informally started planning the next steps for the upcoming yearly contract.

To one of the questions that bordered on – "what is the most important goal for you this year?" he quipped, "To celebrate every day like it's Christmas!" As I egged him on to explain, he laid out his well-being recipes for a happy life. Moments later, as I called for the check, I finally could appreciate what made Charles a happy camper despite the array of production issues he was responsible for.

It came down to three important lessons: (1) don't be serious but give your best; (2) don't take anything personally; and (3) celebrate every day as if it were your last. That conversation had a profound effect on how I went about correcting my habits and value system thereon. I resolved to follow those three steps even in the most difficult circumstances and above all celebrate the opportunity of being a consultant.

Often the stress of traveling and keeping clients happy takes away the fundamental reasons of why one pursues a career in consulting. A better paycheck and the variety found in consulting can be touted as obvious reasons, but they are mostly built on artificial elements that are forgotten as the consultant deals with stressful client situations and unknowns of the next big thing in his career. To enjoy the consulting role, the consultant has to go beyond the short term and material aspects and possess a more holistic approach to consulting and toward life in general. The following affirmations, built on real and healthy foundations, describe that attitude:

1. *I am happy.* I recognize that being happy and finding meaning in life has little to do with my work. I focus on all the good things in my life and extend that goodness to my consulting role.

2. *I trust and give my best.* I will always give my 100 percent and will trust that things will work out. When they don't, I will learn the lessons and move on.

3. *Every situation has meaning.* No matter how ugly or pretty a situation, I witness it as an opportunity for growth. The meaning might not be apparent immediately, but I can connect the dots at a later point.

4. *I smile often and celebrate every day.* There is no reason not to smile and be in high spirits every single day. I have my goals and work toward them by putting my attention on the beauty of fulfilling my responsibilities and deliverables. Success follows automatically.

The aforementioned affirmations are useful for any individual, not just the ones who happen to be in the consulting field. However, by imbibing these qualities, a consultant goes above and beyond his role and creates greater opportunities for success.

So, how does being happy and celebrating every day help the consultant climb the *Pyramid of Expectations*?

1. **Expertise**: Relieved of thoughts and events that are no longer useful, I focus my energy in demonstrating my expertise with high energy and caliber.

2. **Interpersonal skills**: My clients find my sense of enthusiasm infectious. Negotiating with diverse personalities is no more a tiring task.

3. **Delivery excellence**: My deliverables don't carry the burdens of a perfectionist. I have plenty of room to exercise my creative skills. I am grounded in recognizing mistakes and strive to learn from them.

4. **Value**: I add value by being spontaneous and by being present in focusing on my goals. As I trust my abilities to manage any unknowns, I am left with cycles to focus on what really matters to my clients.

5. **Innovation**: Bigger, beautiful things follow me magically, and I make constant leaps in creativity and help my clients innovate. I truly show my customers, the surreal magic of Technology.

The last step of 'celebrating everything' is the most important of all, as it allows the consultant to look at the big picture of life and not sweat the small stuff. This is true for any individual and more so for consultants who tackle the stress of expectations every single day. Being cheerful and happy in the present lays out a good platform for all the good possibilities in the future.

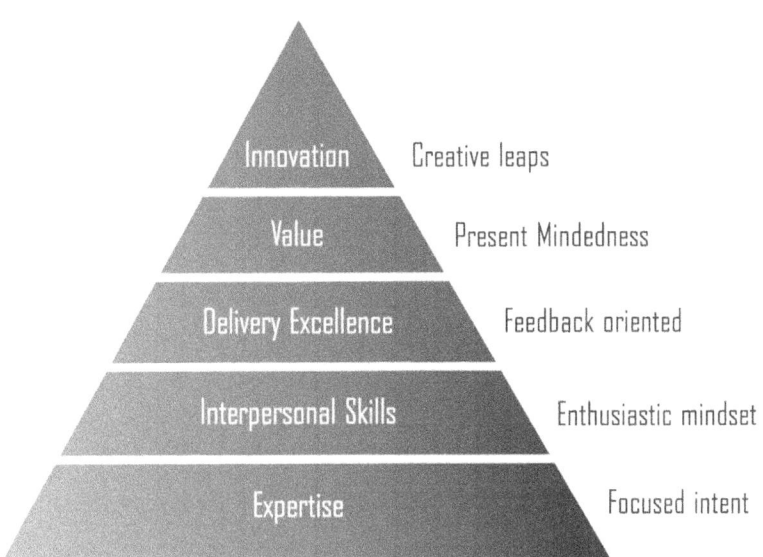

PUTTING THE STEPS INTO PRACTICE

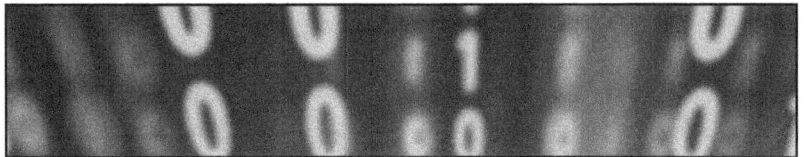

FIVE DAYS OF GLORY

Every consultant is different. We have walked different gardens, smelled different flowers, and stepped on different thorns. Chapters 2 and 3 of this book propose a new reality, one that at the minimum brings forward a decent understanding of client expectations to the consultant in order to be successful. Insights are a blessing but can soon be forgotten making room for old habits of dealing with everyday stress. In the case of consultants, it can just be carrying on with the mundane routine of booking one's flights, researching a new technology, and managing the burdens of desires and expectations.

The purpose of this book is not to demonstrate the elements of a great and successful technology consultant, but rather to showcase how gaining awareness of the world around him enables the consultant to make the most of the presented opportunities. The delight of gaining awareness is akin to unwrapping one gift after another around the Christmas tree. But to receive these gifts, the consultant has to consciously embrace the five steps outlined in this book. So, how does a consultant assemble these five steps on a daily basis and embed them into his consciousness? One method would be to practice each of the five steps as affirmations every day of the workweek.

MONDAY'S AFFIRMATIONS

Today I practice the step of *profiling the client* by holding on to the following affirmations:

1. I will embody the virtues of *curiosity and intrigue.*

2. I will seek to know *two novel aspects* about my client contacts and my clients' business and objectives.

3. I will seek to know *two new client contacts* who can help broaden my network and thereby my understanding of the clients' business and culture.

TUESDAY'S AFFIRMATIONS

Today I practice the step of *using my entrepreneurial spirit* by holding on to the following affirmations:

1. I will embody the virtues of *collaboration and integration*.

2. I will seek to perceive my consulting assignment as a solo business venture. My mantra for today is "*How may I help?*"

3. I will seek to *understand, integrate, and collaborate* with the various colleagues and partners who have common business interests.

WEDNESDAY'S AFFIRMATIONS

Today I practice the step of *adding polish to my execution* by holding on to the following affirmations:

1. I will embody the virtues of *finesse and professionalism*.

2. I will seek to self-examine the *professionalism and craft* of my interaction with clients and colleagues.

3. I will seek to add a *unique personal and lasting touch* to all my deliverables, something for the client to remember me by.

THURSDAY'S AFFIRMATIONS

Today I practice the step of *going social with my expertise* by holding on to the following affirmations:

1. I will embody the virtues of *sharing and learning.*

2. I will seek to *record all the valuable insights* I absorb from this engagement in a social medium.

3. As an earnest student, I will seek to keep *an open mind to learn at least two new things* from the world around me.

FRIDAY'S AFFIRMATIONS

Today I practice the step of *celebrating everything* by holding on to the following affirmations:

1. I will embody the virtues of *joyfulness and carefreeness.*

2. I will seek to *laugh, embrace uncertainty, and not take myself seriously.*

3. I will *trust and go beyond billing and getting billed,* knowing that the universe is on my side.

IT TRENDS AND THE CHANGING ROLE OF THE CONSULTANT

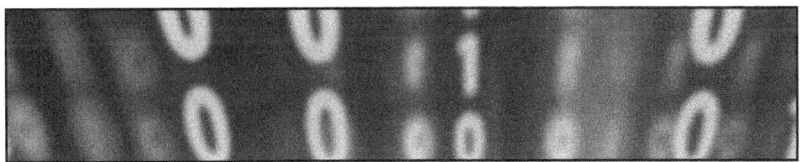

At the time of writing this book, technology is living up to Ray Kurzweil's predictions from his proposed law of accelerating returns. According to Kurzweil, the rate of change and innovation in technology tends to increase exponentially. So, according to the law of accelerating returns – "we won't experience 100 years of progress in the 21st century – it will be more like 20,000 years of progress".

The law of accelerating returns is proving to be correct. IT organizations across the world are currently in the process of reacting to the massive disruptions caused by Cloud computing, proliferation of new form factors such as mobile phones and tablets and a generation of workers that rely on Social computing as a primary form of communication. As technology amplifies human effort, there is an active collective force – call it consciousness or evolution, that continuously re-innovates itself to solve problems. This force is active, nonstop and trudges forward at the rate presented by the law of accelerating returns.

As much as IT organizations prepare themselves to meet these changes head-on, there are technological gaps that remain unconquered for every business. These gaps collectively present themselves as competitive threats or as competitive edges depending on which side of the coin businesses find themselves on.

So, how is the value of a consultant impacted while businesses deal with these technological pressures that arise from these gaps? Simply put, a consultant needs to align himself with the specific IT challenges the business is trying to solve. It might be more difficult than that, as most IT organizations either lose sight of their IT goals to bureaucracy or delude themselves in believing that they are on the right path. For a consultant, the challenge then becomes multi-fold.

Clients expect consultants to turn their technological needs into competitive edges by giving them the best practices around implementation and maintenance. It is expected that a consultant make every penny invested in him count, and at the same time ensure the timelines and deliverables are met. Never before was a time where the demands on IT have been so huge and dynamic, that it invariably impacts the consultant. Should a consultant then, play it safe and take the client's side and speak the client's language, or should he vehemently propose the direction that would best serve the client? The answer unfortunately is not straightforward, and has layers of dependency – right from the nature of the client engagement to the vested interests of the consultant and his employer.

So the best approach for the consultant in any case, is to become the bridge of the awareness and opportunities, other than meeting the specific goals of his consulting engagement. The consultant can roll up his sleeves and execute his tasks in the most efficient manner and yet not miss the opportunity of guiding his client in the right direction. In order to do so, a consultant can once again tap into the *Pyramid of Expectations* to create a win-win situation. The next section gives a map of how the consultant can achieve this task and be successful, based on the Pyramid.

LEADING THE CUSTOMER THROUGH MASSIVE DISRUPTIONS

Expertise: One of the core elements of my expertise is the ability to comprehensively understand my client's business, competition, IT goals and the opportunities to keep up with the current trends. I strive to help the client to be factually aware of the different approaches (using for example – case studies), explain the pros and cons, but will let the client validate and decide on the final approach.

Interpersonal skills: I am able to present my views on contradictory opinions, deal with stalemates and negotiate diverse perspectives based on my awareness of computing trends. I strive to be honest in my assessment, without rigidly holding on to my opinions.

Delivery excellence: I make every effort to lead the customer in the direction using validated, industry wide best practices. I possess a professional network of colleagues and friends who can I tap into to help me in the right direction. From this gathered awareness, I outline a detailed plan of my tasks to demonstrate my action points.

Value: Every element of my client interaction carries the best interests of the client. I clearly articulate the value of engaging my services, using clearly defined shared goals. The Client can clearly map my value to their goals and can intuitively understand that I have brought them closer in meeting their goals and challenges.

Innovation: Through my work, I prepare my client's business to gain competitive edge in the market through technology. Even if that is unapparent, the client appreciates my hard work and my intention of steering the engagement in that direction.

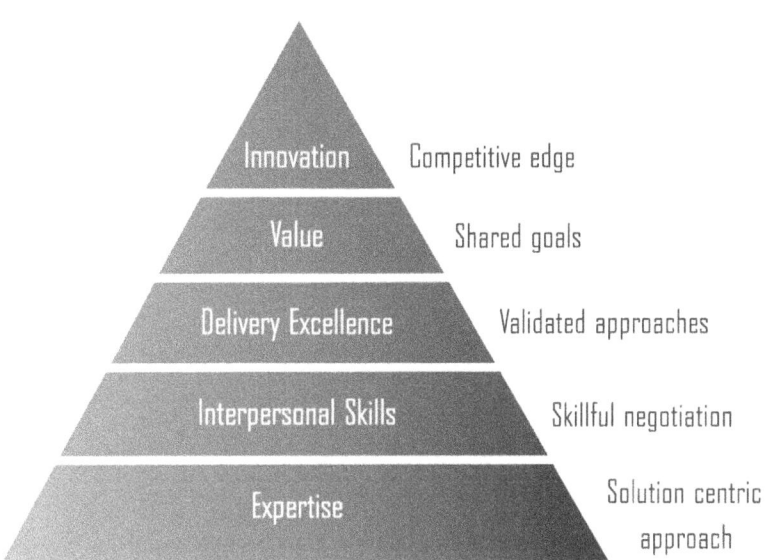

.